Copyright Notice © Scrapbooking Coach
All Rights Reserved

No part of this book or any of its contents may be reproduced, copied, modified or adapted without the prior written consent of the author, unless otherwise indicated for stand-alone materials.

The author retains the right to change this guide at any time. This guide is for information purposes only and the author doesn't accept any responsibilities for any liabilities resulting from the use of this information. The reader assumes all responsibility for the use of the information herein.

Table of Contents

Introduction	3
1 Photo Layouts	4
2 Photo Layouts	21
3 & 4 Photo Layouts	36
Themed Layouts	47
11.5" x 8" Layouts	75

Ready To Get More Creative?

Welcome to **"525 New and Creative Scrapbook Sketches!"**

I've created the sketches inside this book so you can tell your story in a creative way and develop your creativity so you can create beautiful pages that you'll love, for years to come.

Each sketch takes you on a wonderful, creative journey.

Whether you're following the structure of the photos or going deeper and adding splashes of paint or layers of texture, I want to inspire you to take your scrapbooking to the next level and be proud of what you create every time.

Be sure to join us on Instagram and Facebook and become a part of a truly supportive and inspirational community.

Finally - if this is your first time using one of our sketches books, be sure to check out Volumes 1, 2 and 3 covering double page layouts, more themed sketches and lots lots more!

Anna Lyons

From The Desk Of Anna Lyons
ScrapbookingCoach.com

1 Photo Layouts

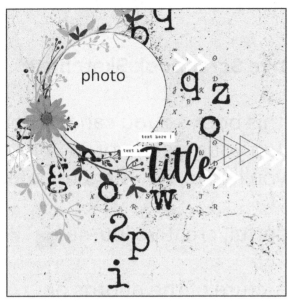
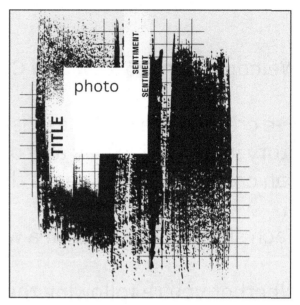
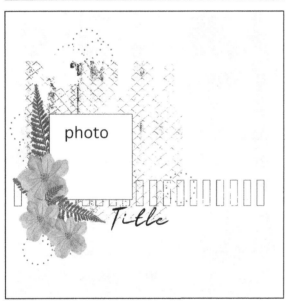

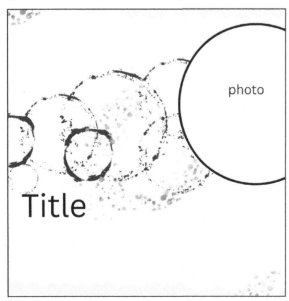
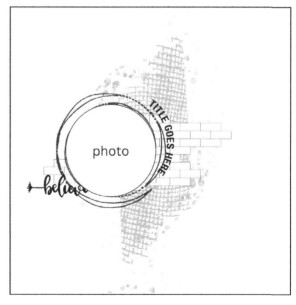

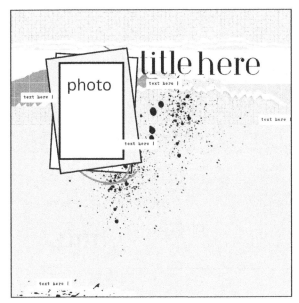

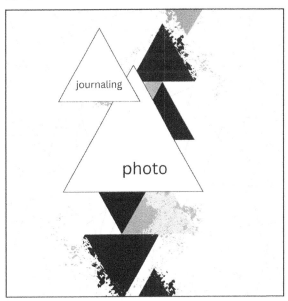
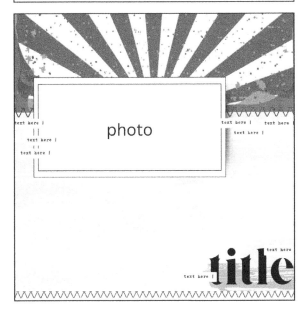
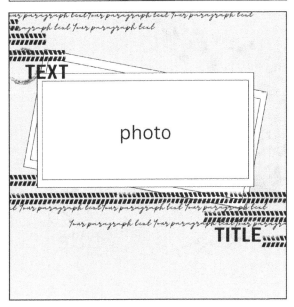

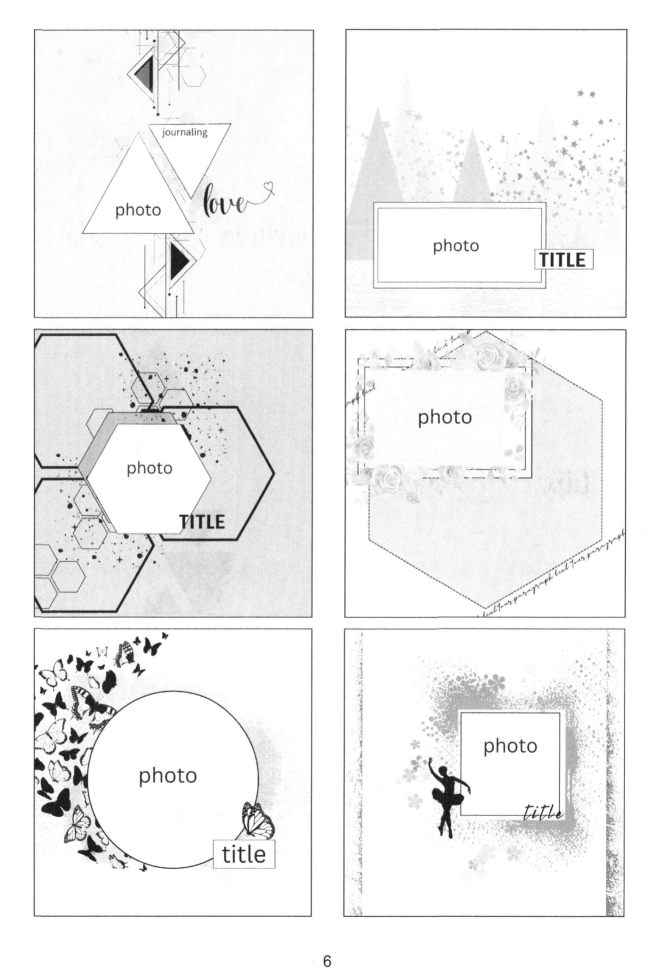

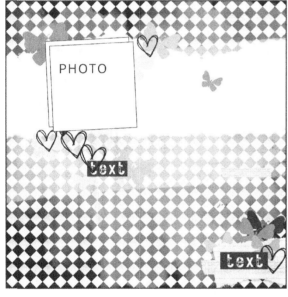
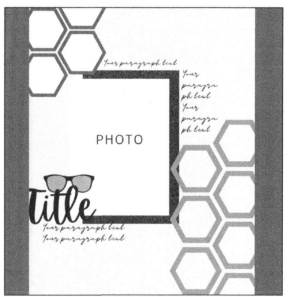
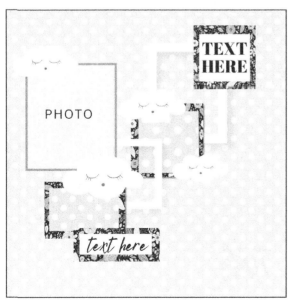

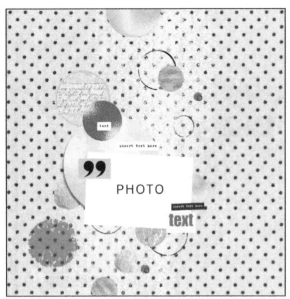

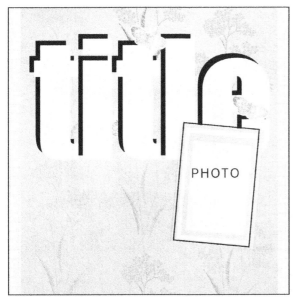

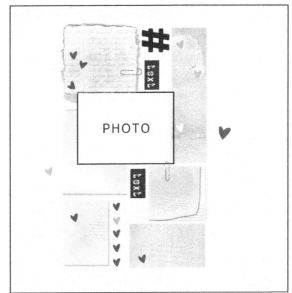

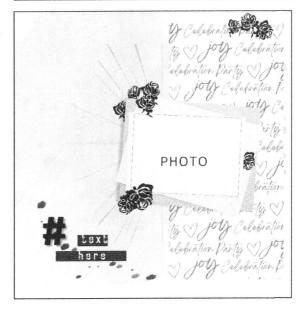

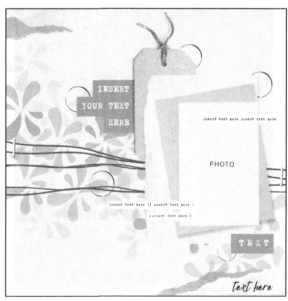

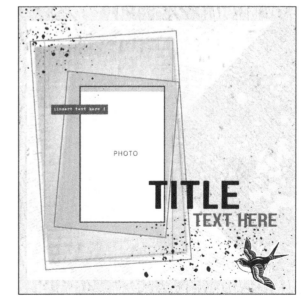

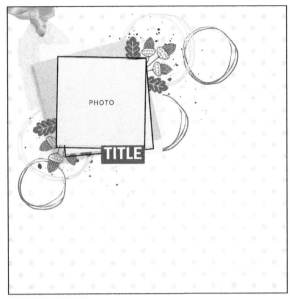

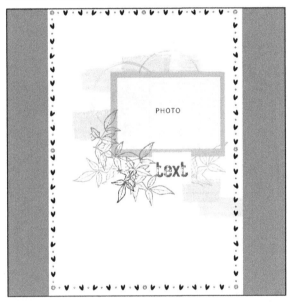

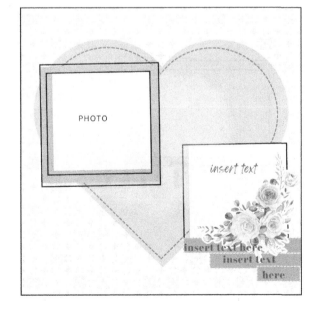

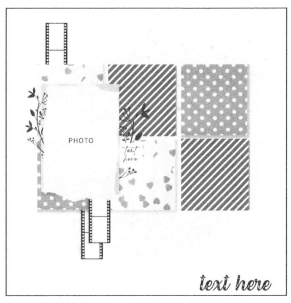

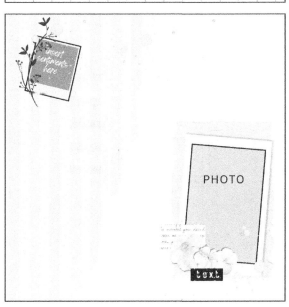

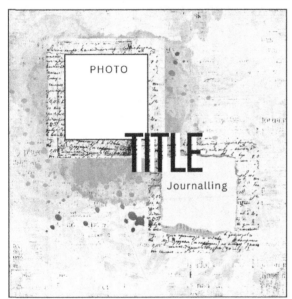

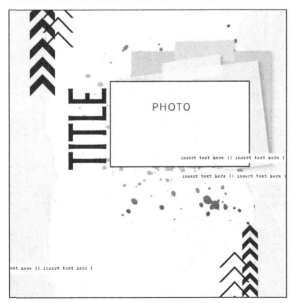

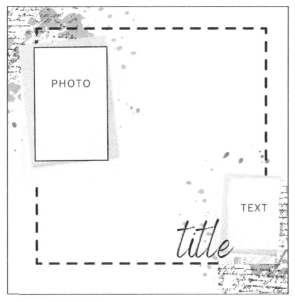

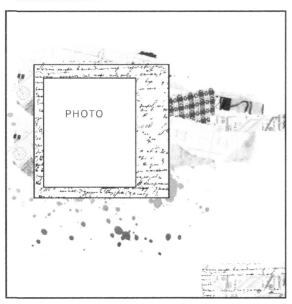

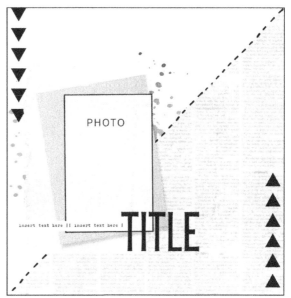

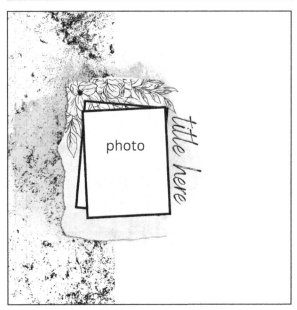

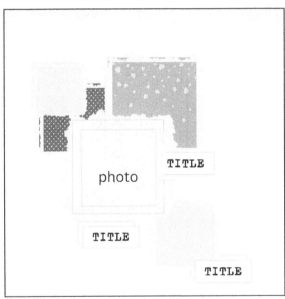

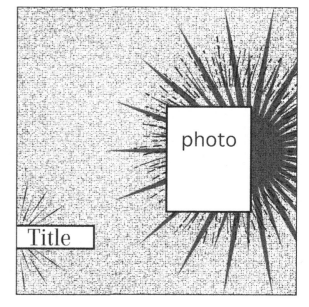

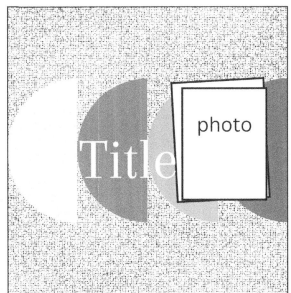

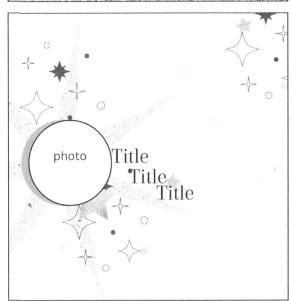
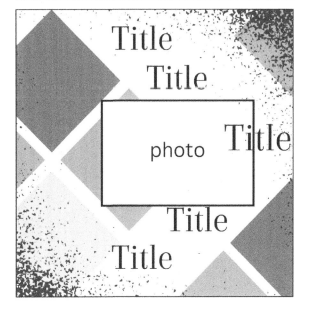

2 Photo Layouts

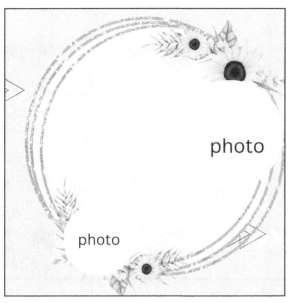

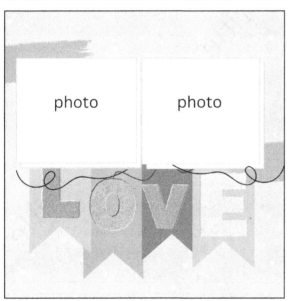
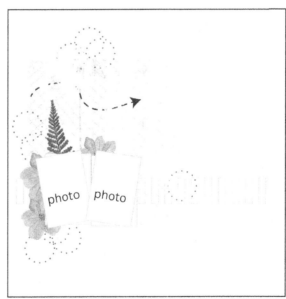

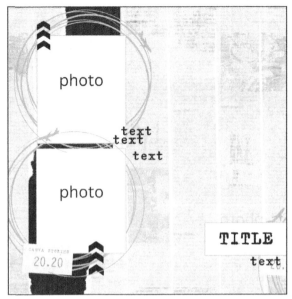
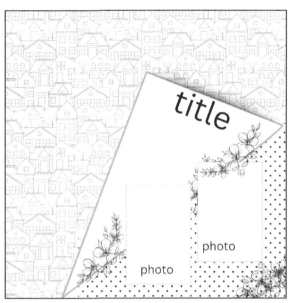
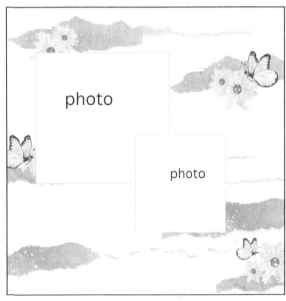
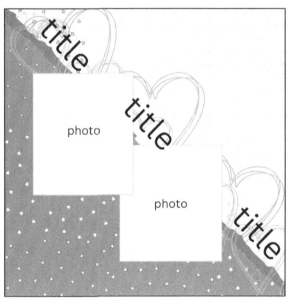

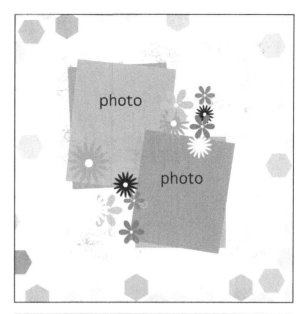
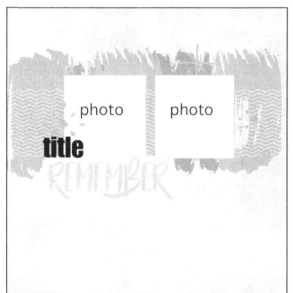
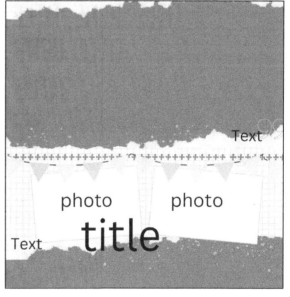
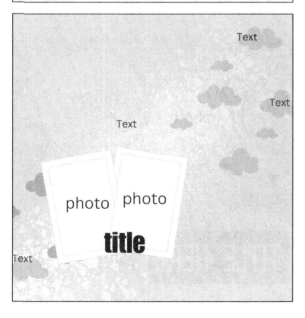
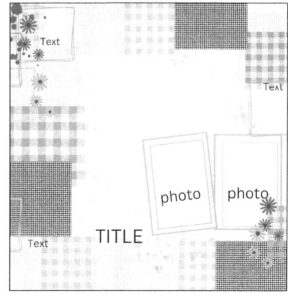

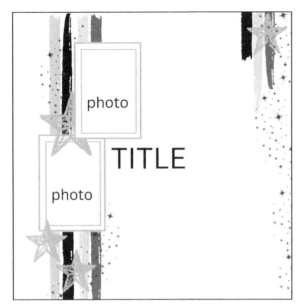
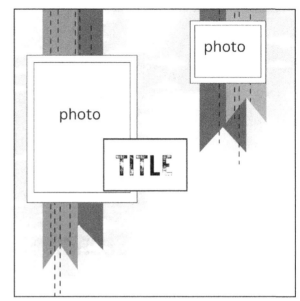

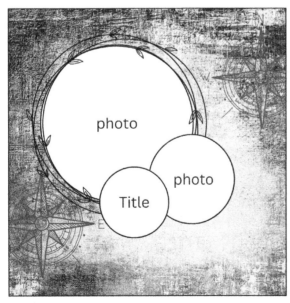
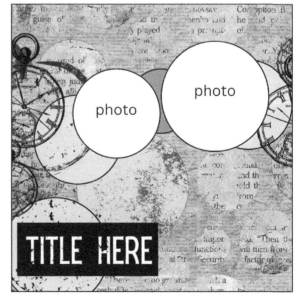

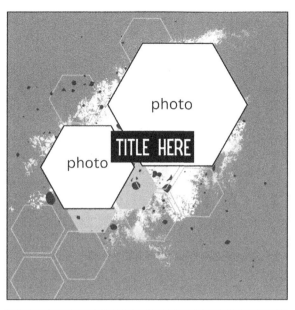
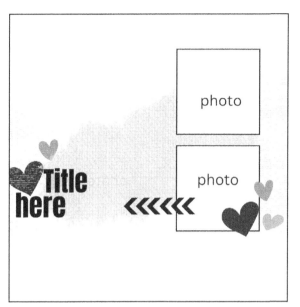

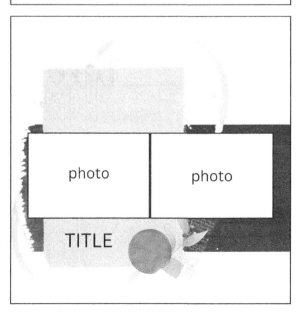

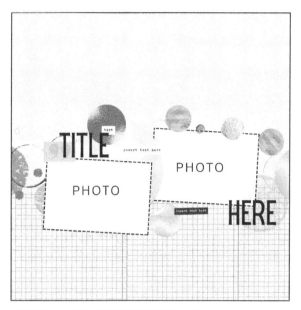

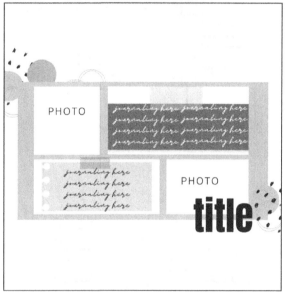

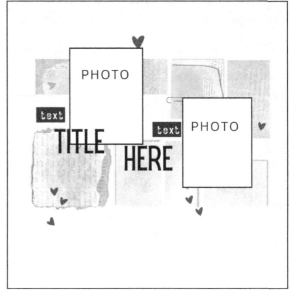
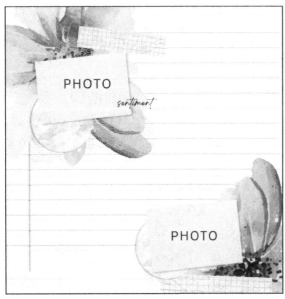

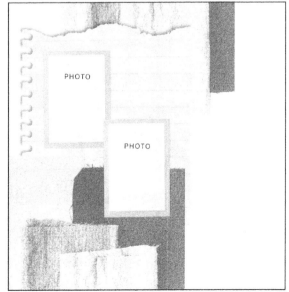

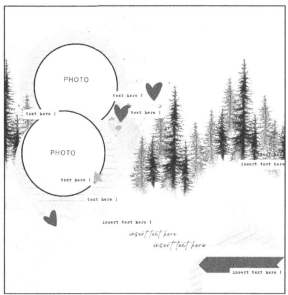

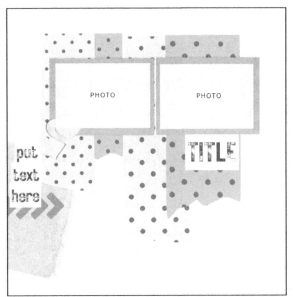
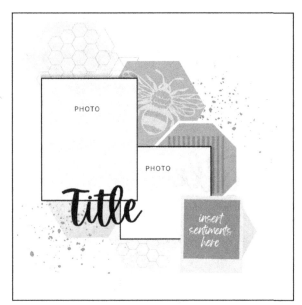

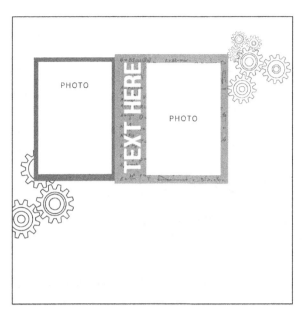
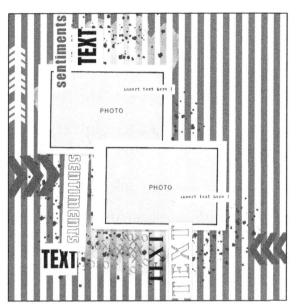

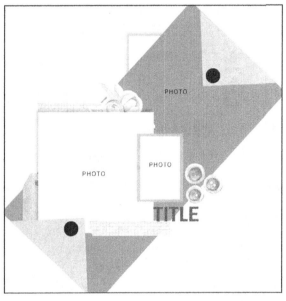
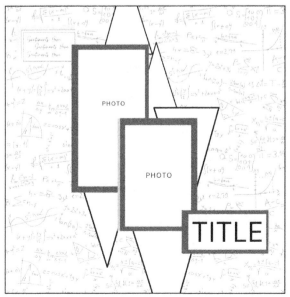

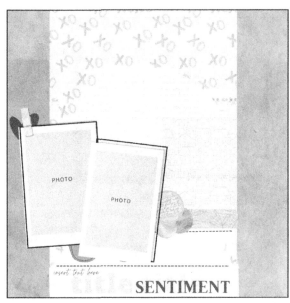

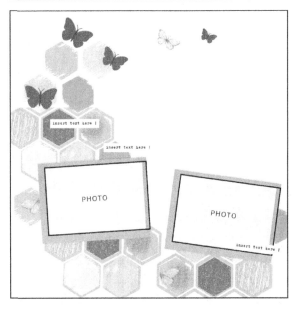

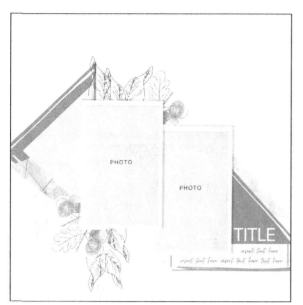
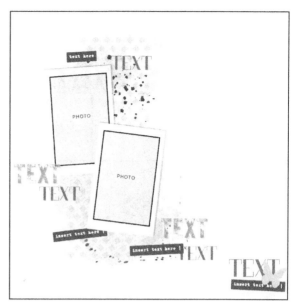
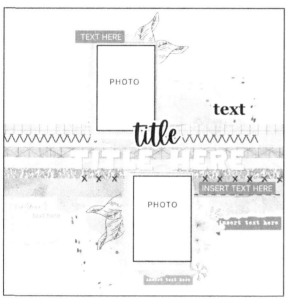

3 & 4 Photo Layouts

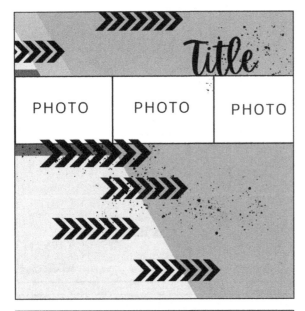

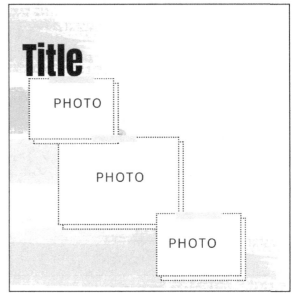

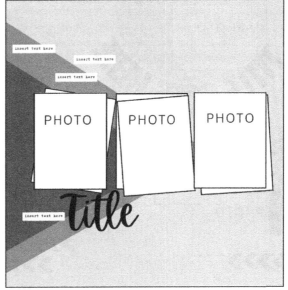
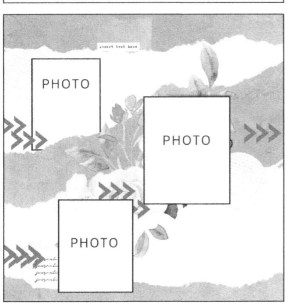
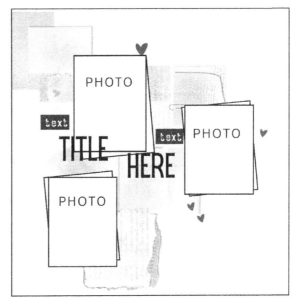

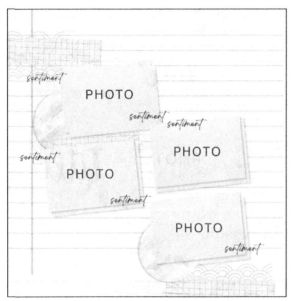

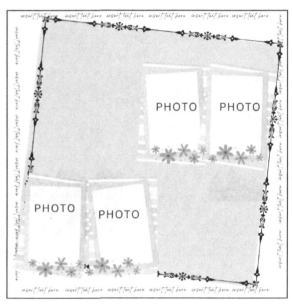
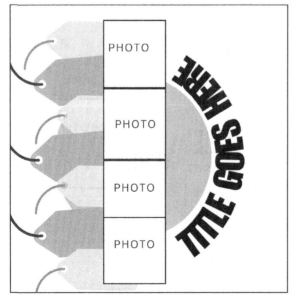

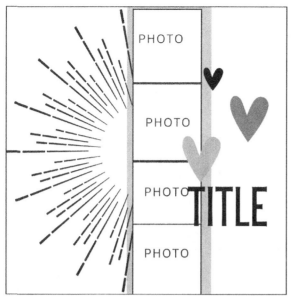

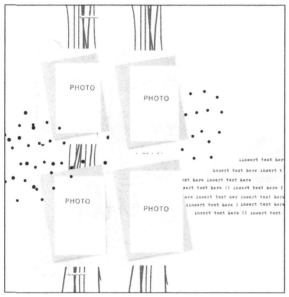
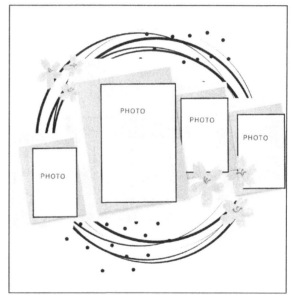
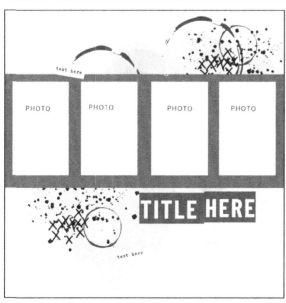

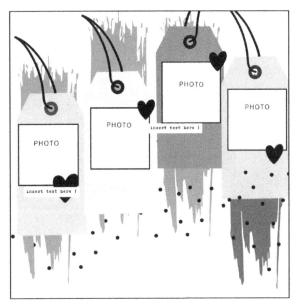
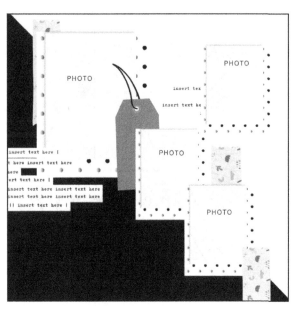
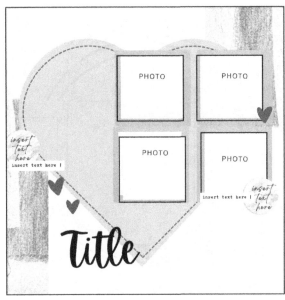

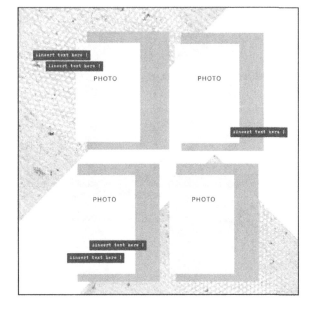

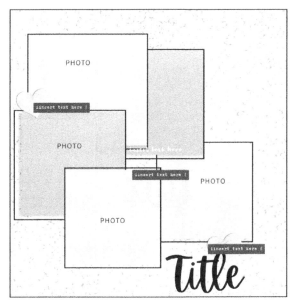

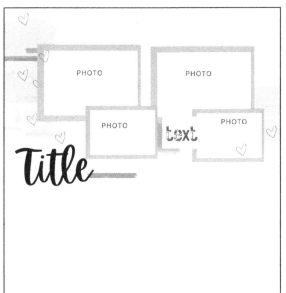
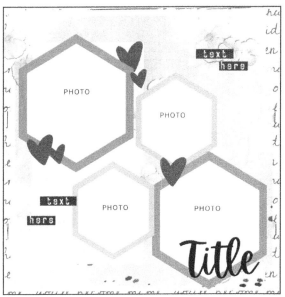

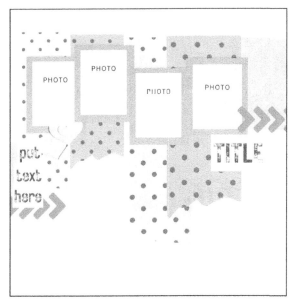

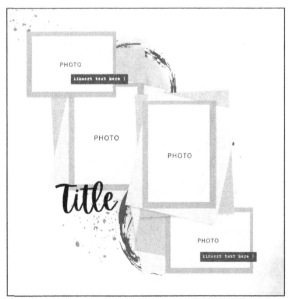

 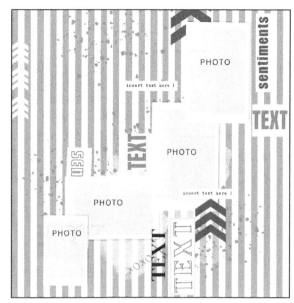

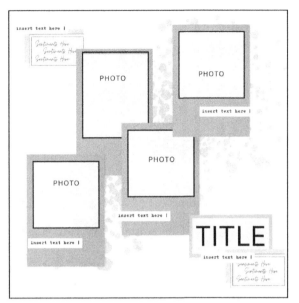

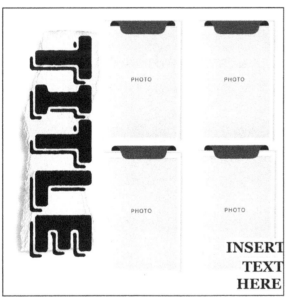

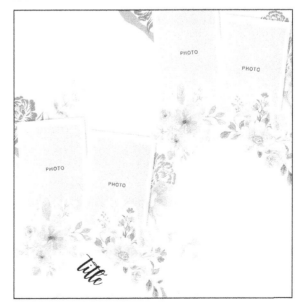

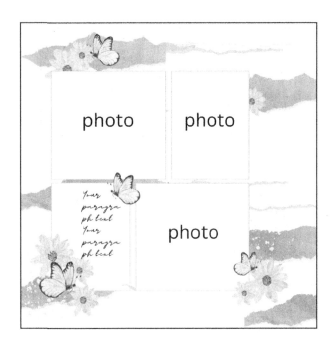

Themed Layouts

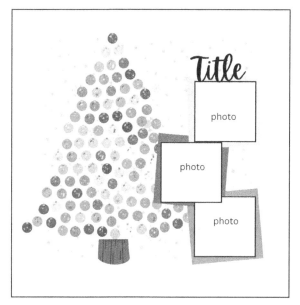

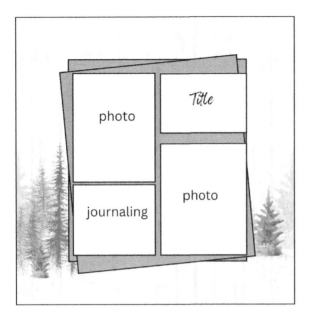
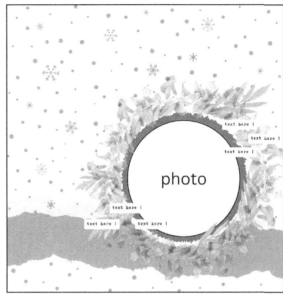

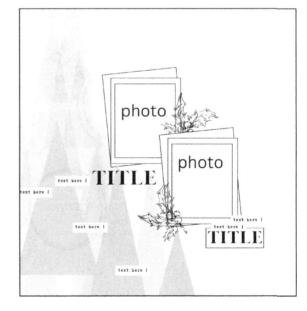

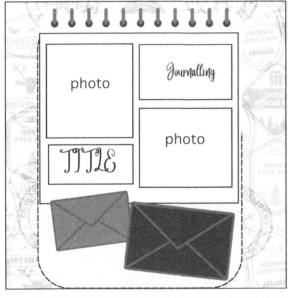

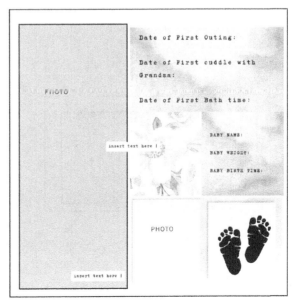

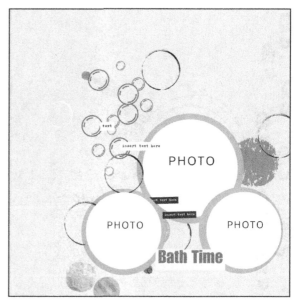
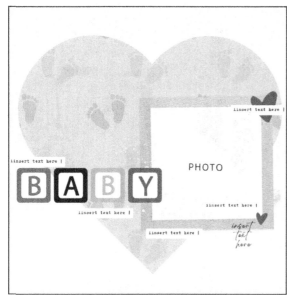

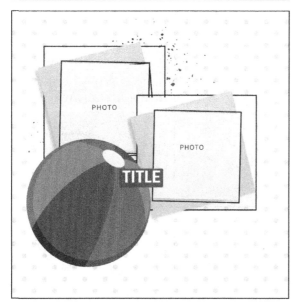

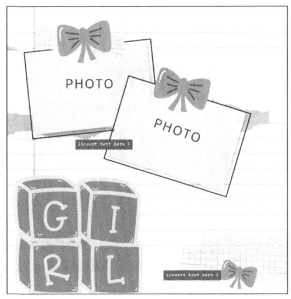

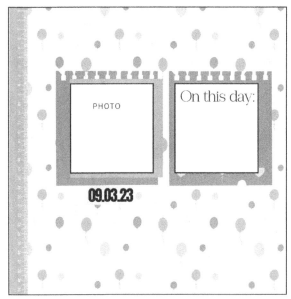

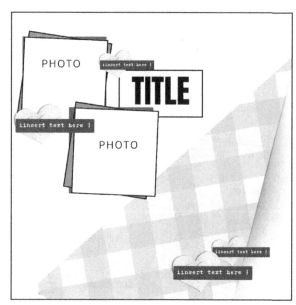

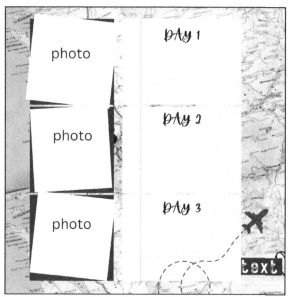

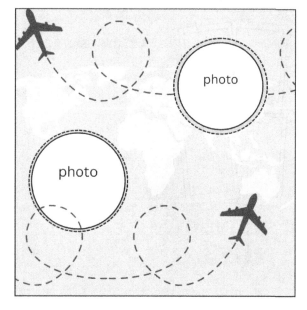

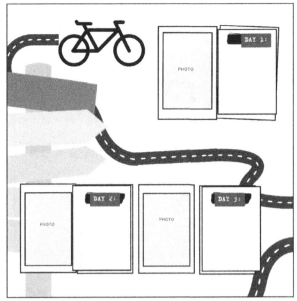

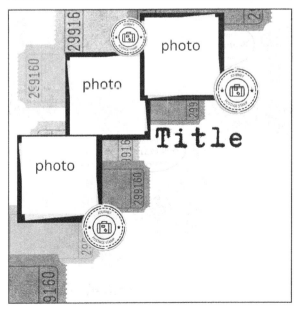

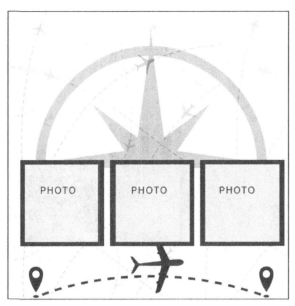

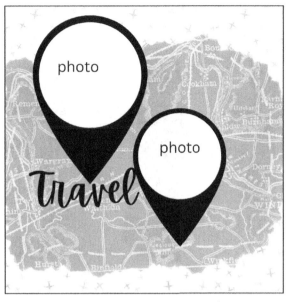
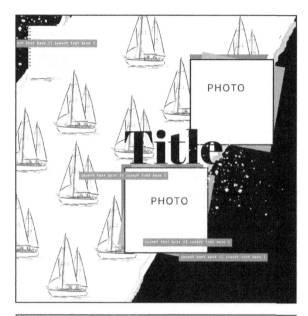

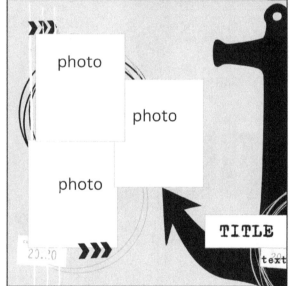

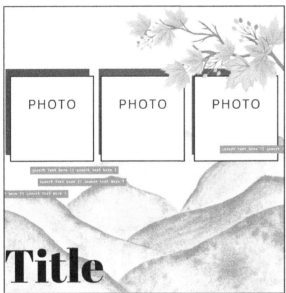

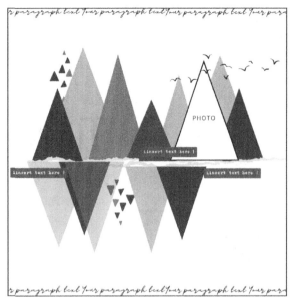

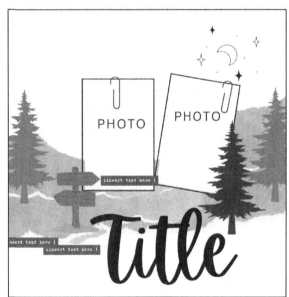

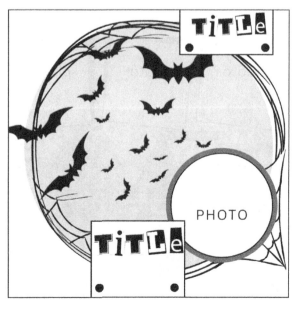

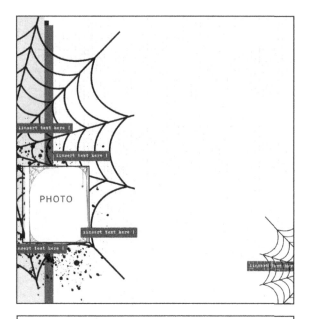

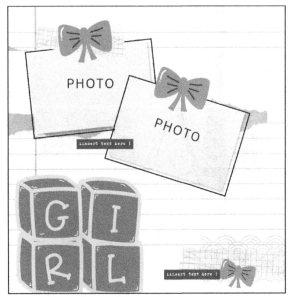

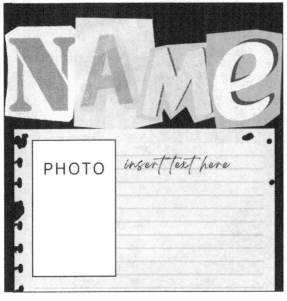

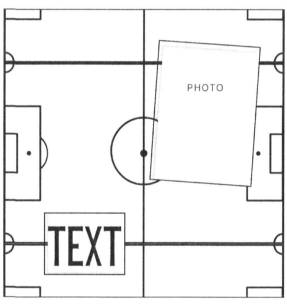

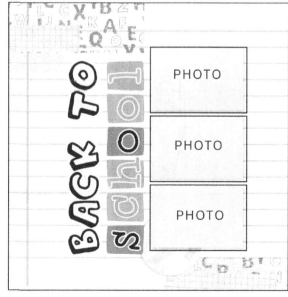

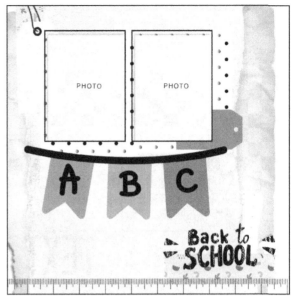
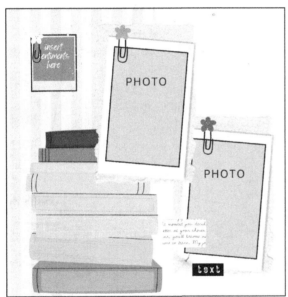
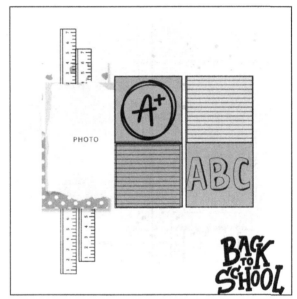

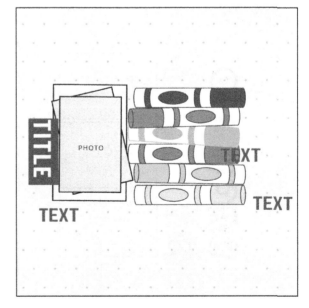

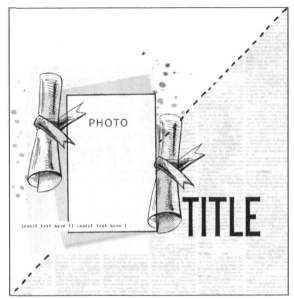

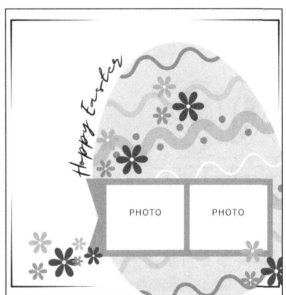

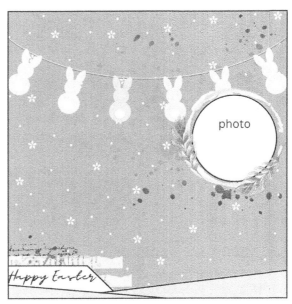

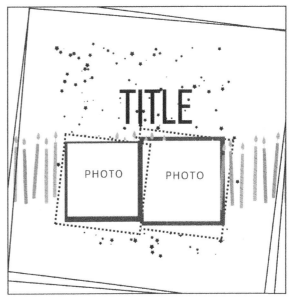

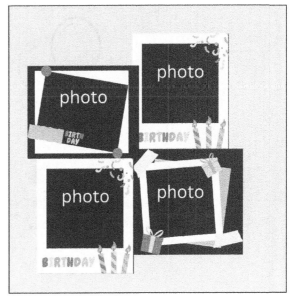

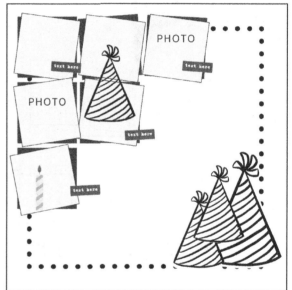

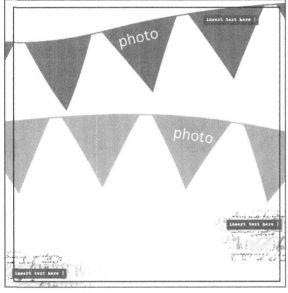

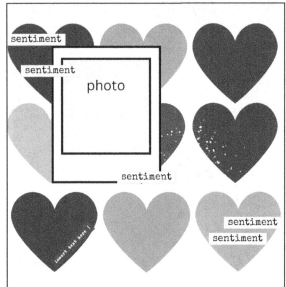

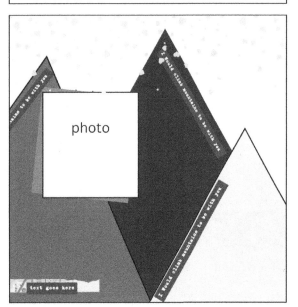

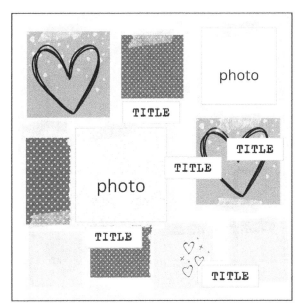

11.5" x 8" Layouts

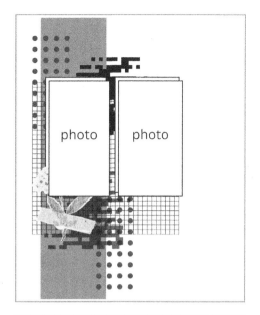
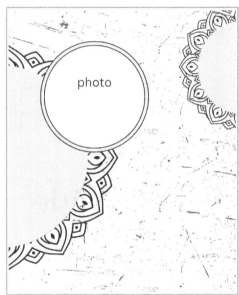
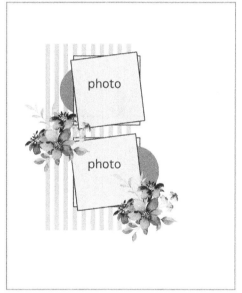

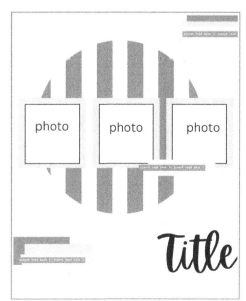

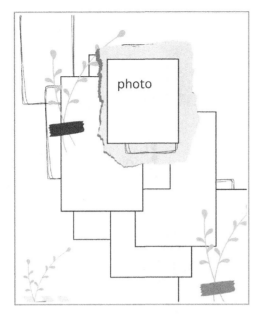
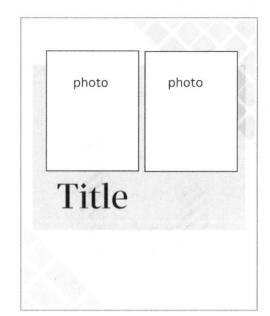

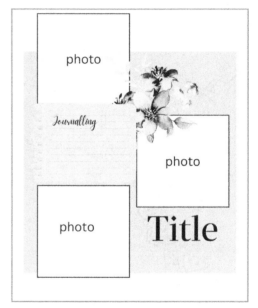
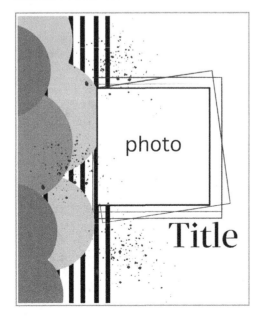
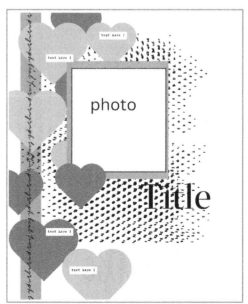

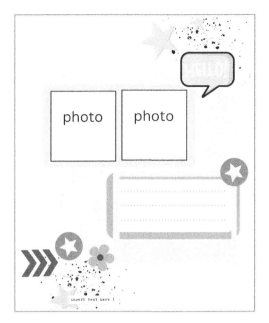

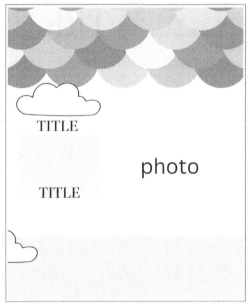
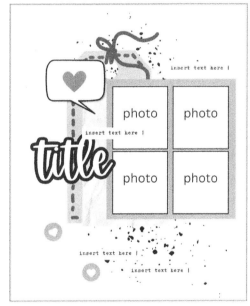
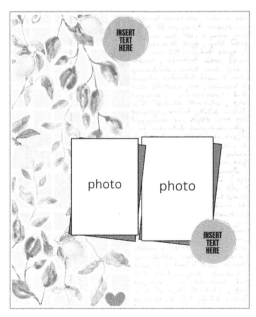

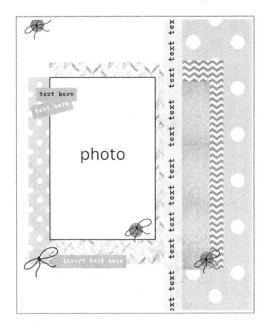

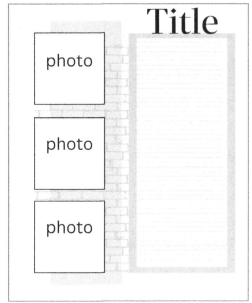
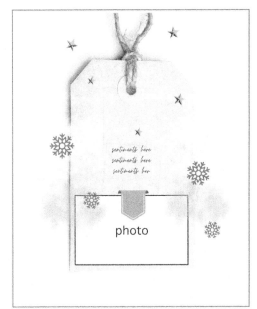
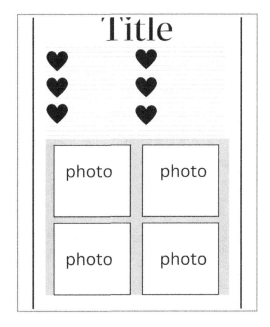

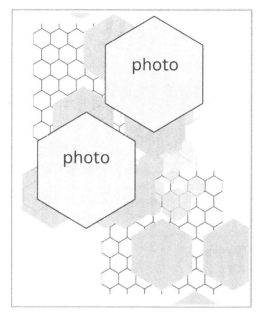
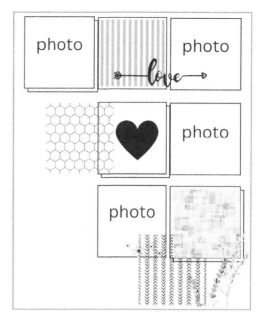
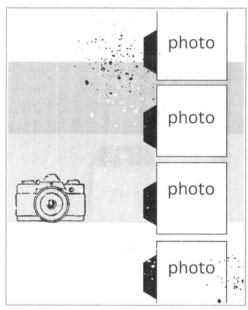

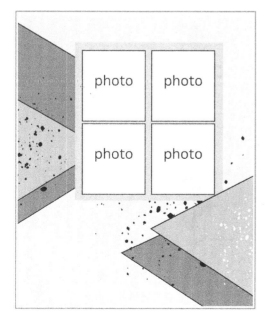
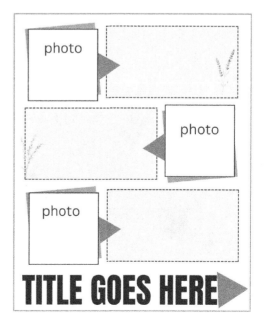

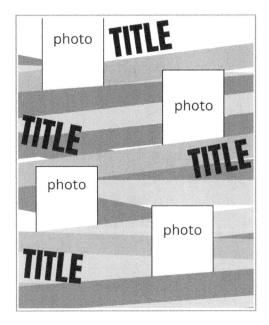
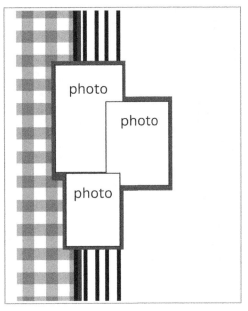
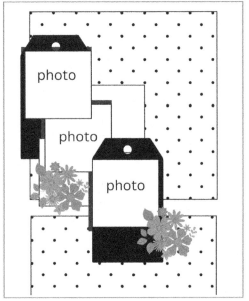

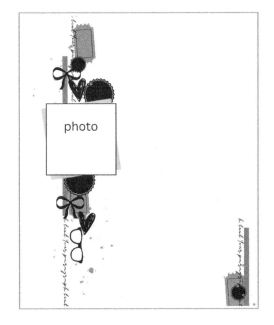

80

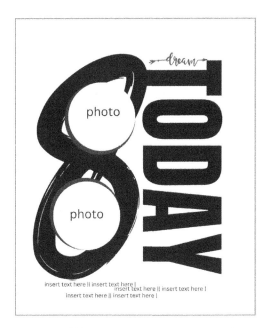
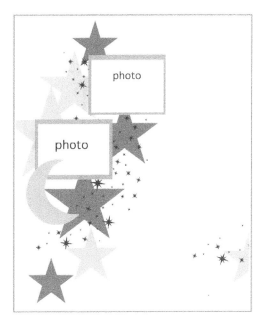

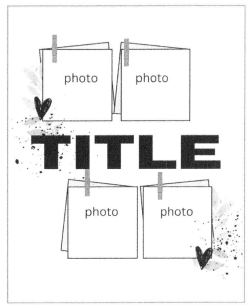
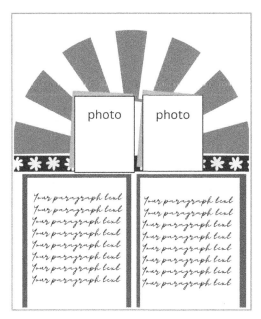
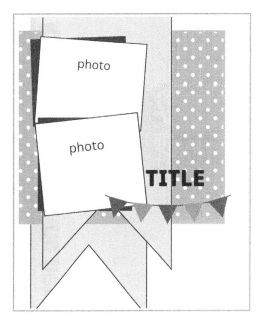

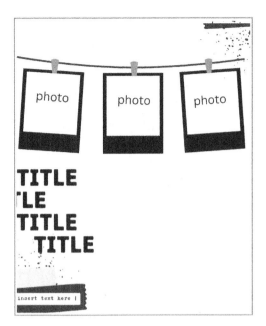
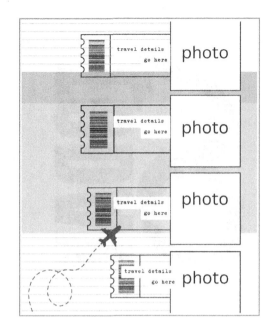

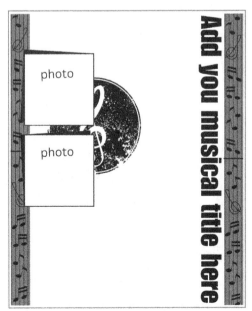

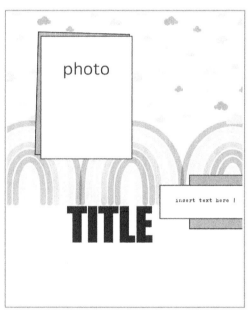
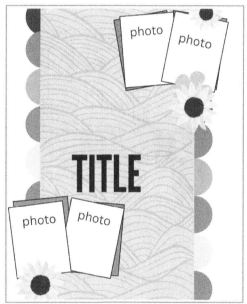

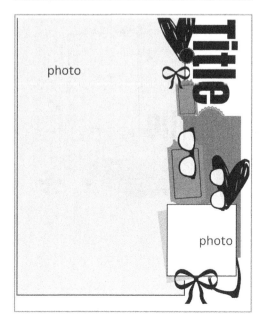

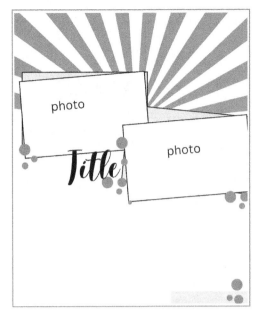

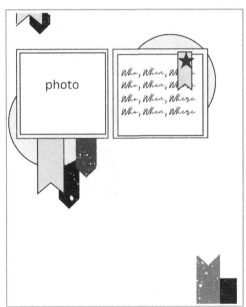

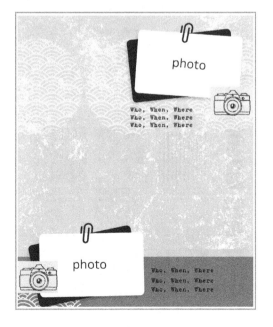

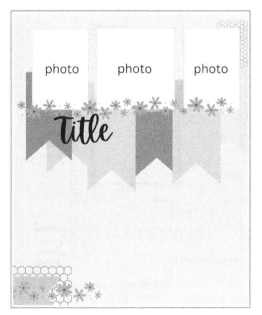

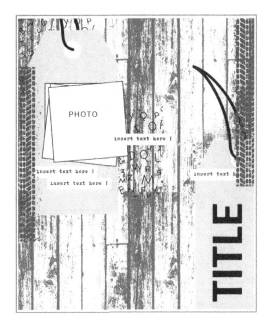
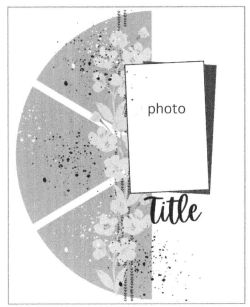

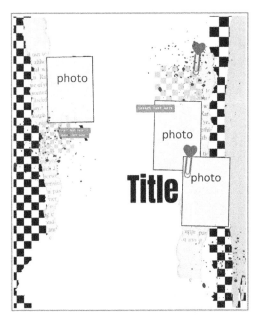
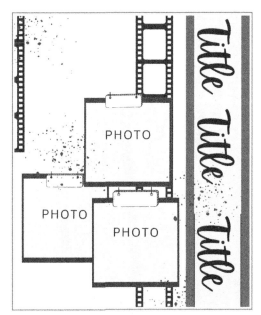

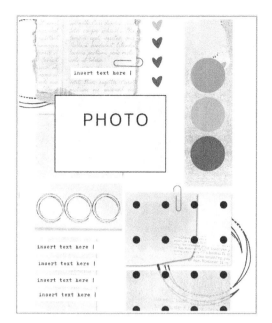

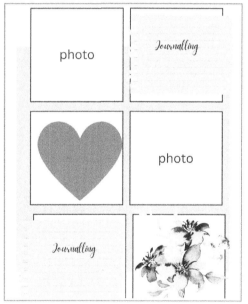
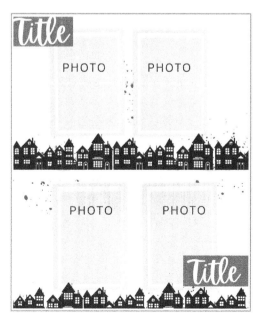

Made in the USA
Coppell, TX
14 December 2024

42406817R00050